Chadwick Friends of the Library

In Celebration of the Birthday of

Olivia Maxson

This Book has been

Presented to

Leavenworth Library

by

The Maxson Family

December 9th, 2009

EXTREME ENVIRONMENTAL THREATS™

NOT ENOUGH TO DRINK

Pollution, Drought, and Tainted Water Supplies

Laura La Bella

ROSEN
PUBLISHING®

New York

Published in 2009 by The Rosen Publishing Group, Inc.
29 East 21st Street, New York, NY 10010

First Edition

Library of Congress Cataloging-in-Publication Data

La Bella, Laura.
Not enough to drink : pollution, drought, and tainted water supplies / Laura La Bella.
    p. cm.—(Extreme environmental threats)
Includes bibliographical references and index.
ISBN-13: 978-1-4358-5020-0 (library binding)
ISBN-13: 978-1-4358-5376-8 (pbk)
ISBN-13: 978-1-4358-5380-5 (6 pack)
1. Water-supply—Juvenile literature. 2. Water—Pollution—Juvenile literature.
3. Droughts—Juvenile literature. I. Title.
TD348.L32 2009
363.6'1—dc22
2008016737

Manufactured in Malaysia

BC 23096

On the cover: A kayaker trying to enjoy a day on the river is slowed by floating trash and debris. **Title page:** A rainwater diversion channel runs dry as the surrounding desert community of Albuquerque, New Mexico, suffers the effects of a drought and increasingly limited water resources.

Contents

INTRODUCTION   4

1   FRESHWATER SUPPLY AND DEMAND   8

2   POLLUTING OUR FRESHWATER RESOURCES   18

3   GLOBAL WARMING AND OTHER STRESSES
    ON FRESHWATER   28

4   CONSERVATION VS. GROWTH   37

5   IMPROVING AND PROTECTING
    FRESHWATER SUPPLIES   45

GLOSSARY   56

FOR MORE INFORMATION   57

FOR FURTHER READING   59

BIBLIOGRAPHY   60

INDEX   62

INTRODUCTION

Streams, ponds, and rivers are among the few sources of freshwater for people and wildlife.

On a hot day, when the sun is beating down, there is nothing more satisfying than a tall glass of clean, clear, ice-cold water. Water is an essential element for life. Both people and wildlife need it to survive. But what if someday, you can't just go to your kitchen to get a glass of water from the sink because your freshwater supply is gone? The idea is not as far-fetched as you might think. While more than 70 percent of our planet is covered by water, it may surprise you to know that the type of water we need to survive, called freshwater, is in limited supply.

How limited? Of all the surface water that covers the planet, only 3 percent is freshwater. Of that 3 percent, about two-thirds of it is frozen in glaciers and polar ice caps. According to NationalGeographic.com, if a one-dollar bill represented all of the surface water on the planet, less than half of one penny would represent the world's supply of freshwater. That means only about 0.3 percent of all the water on Earth's surface—found in rivers, lakes, and wetlands, which includes ponds, marshes, swamps, and bogs—is safe and usable for drinking, showering, watering our crops, and powering our industries. The rest of the planet's water is salt water, which is water found in an ocean or a sea. This water contains salt, or sodium chloride, which makes it unusable—even unsafe—for drinking.

The world's supply of freshwater is small. It's also in danger of being depleted. Water has many uses, and because of this, people have altered freshwater habitats more than any other on Earth. We've built dams to block the natural flow of rivers, controlling the flow of water to towns, cities, and farmlands. We've drained wetlands to build shopping malls, business complexes, and housing developments. We contaminate our waterways with trash, chemicals, and other pollutants. We use more water than we really need to do everyday tasks such as washing our dishes, brushing our teeth, and watering our lawns. And we've built entire communities in desert areas that have limited access to freshwater. All of this strains our existing water supply.

The reality is that there is essentially no more freshwater on the planet today than there was two thousand years ago, when Earth's population was less than 3 percent of its current size. Right now, more than 5.5 billion people around the world rely on the same amount of water that existed just a few thousand years ago.

While the demand for freshwater is growing faster and faster, there is good news: freshwater is one of the very few natural resources that is renewable. That means freshwater can be replenished, and there are many companies and organizations worldwide that are fighting to preserve rivers, lakes, and wetlands so that they will continue to provide water for all of the many ways we use it.

FRESHWATER SUPPLY AND DEMAND

The Colorado River is one of the biggest sources of freshwater to communities in the western United States.

There are two kinds of water on Earth: salt water and freshwater. Salt water, found in oceans and seas, contains salt. In every liter of salt water there is approximately thirty-five grams of salt. This high level of salt makes the water unusable for drinking, showering, or watering crops. People can only drink up to two cups of salt water before they begin to get sick. Our bodies are not used to filtering and getting rid of the amounts of salt found in salt water, so we cannot rely on this water to sustain us. By contrast, freshwater has very limited amounts of salt in it, which is why it's referred to as "fresh" water.

Freshwater is located all over the planet. It can be found in rivers, lakes, ponds, marshes, swamps, and bogs. Freshwater also fills streams and reservoirs. It collects underground in aquifers and is frozen in glaciers, ice caps, and ice shelves. Each of these bodies of water, big and small, is part of a distinct ecosystem. A freshwater ecosystem is a community of plants, animals, and smaller organisms that live, feed, reproduce, and interact in the same area or environment. According to the Environmental Protection Agency (EPA), there are seven major groups of organisms known to live in freshwater ecosystems. These groups include vertebrates (fish, amphibians, reptiles, birds, and mammals), invertebrates (worms and mollusks), plants, algae, fungi, bacteria, and viruses. These organisms cannot survive in salt water, so they find their homes in freshwater.

Freshwater is one of the world's few renewable resources, along with oxygen and timber. These are considered renewable resources because they can be replenished through a natural process in the environment. Oxygen is a gas that is given off by all plants, and so it continually fills the atmosphere. Trees can be planted and grown to add more oxygen to the air and to replace timber that has been cut down.

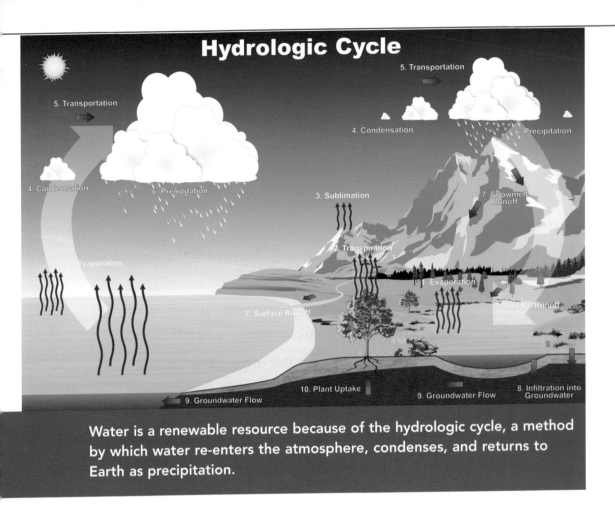

Hydrologic Cycle

5. Transportation

5. Transportation

4. Condensation

6. Precipitation

4. Condensation

6. Precipitation

3. Sublimation

7. Snowmelt Runoff

2. Transpiration

1. Evaporation

1. Evaporation

7. Surface Runoff

Surface Runoff

10. Plant Uptake

8. Infiltration into Groundwater

9. Groundwater Flow

9. Groundwater Flow

Water is a renewable resource because of the hydrologic cycle, a method by which water re-enters the atmosphere, condenses, and returns to Earth as precipitation.

THE HYDROLOGIC CYCLE

Freshwater is replenished through a process called the hydrologic cycle. This process recycles the planet's freshwater supply over and over again. According to the Foundation for Water and Energy Education, the hydrologic cycle, also known as the water cycle, begins when the sun's energy heats water and causes it to evaporate from oceans, rivers, and lakes. This evaporated water is called vapor. Vapor rises into the atmosphere, where it cools and condenses. As the water vapor condenses, it clings to fine particles in the air such as dust, pollen, and pollutants. This step is called condensation.

When enough vapor attaches itself to these fine particles, a cloud is formed. As the air gets more and more moist from an increase in vapor, the vapor droplets that form the clouds grow larger and larger. They eventually grow so large that the atmosphere can no longer hold them, so the clouds release the droplets into the sky. This is called precipitation. Depending on how cold the temperature is in the atmosphere, these droplets can fall as rain, snow, sleet, or hail. This is how freshwater is renewed.

When these droplets reach the ground, they can collect in rivers and lakes, or they are absorbed in the ground, replenishing our groundwater supply, which is one of the world's largest storages of freshwater. Each time a molecule of water goes through the hydrologic cycle, it is cleaned, or purified, so that it can be used over and over again by plants, animals, and people.

THE GROWING DEMAND FOR FRESHWATER

Even though the water cycle continually renews the freshwater supply on our planet, that doesn't mean that this supply is endless. Freshwater can become nonrenewable if it is used at a rate greater than that at which the environment can replenish it. This is why freshwater supplies are in grave danger. Right now, the demand for freshwater is growing faster than its supply and replenishment.

As the world's human population grows, it places greater demand on our supply of freshwater. According to the Nature Conservancy, nearly three billion people live in the world's cities today. That number is expected to grow to more than five billion by the year 2050. While the demand for water by agriculture and industry seems to have leveled off, the growing population means that more water will be needed to support the population in the future—possibly as much as 70 percent more than what we use today.

Environmentalists have long been concerned about the stress that the growing population will place upon our natural resources. Freshwater is not the only resource at risk. Mining also depletes many of our natural resources, including metals such as ore and nickel, and oil used to power our cars. And the continued use of cut timber to make paper or wood products, like furniture, is leading to deforestation and loss of invaluable carbon-absorbing trees. While these are major environmental concerns, according to Lawrence Smith, president of the Population Institute, a lack of fresh, clean water is our most immediate concern. "If the water goes, the

The world's population is expected to grow to more than five billion by 2050, placing extraordinary demands on our freshwater supply.

species goes," Smith said in an interview with CNN.com about the effects of overpopulation. "The accessibility of water, the competition for water, the availability of water is going to be a major, major threat."

As a result, water conservation has become an important issue worldwide. Water conservation is simply using less water in your everyday life. It's the most cost-effective and environmentally sound way to reduce our individual and collective demand for water. The EPA has started a new program called WaterSense. In order to make it easier for Americans to save water and protect

Your Water Usage

Do you know how much water it takes to perform some of the everyday activities that take place in the average home? Check out this list below. It takes:

- 2 to 5 gallons (7.5–19 liters) of water to brush your teeth.
- ˙50 gallons (189 l) of water to wash one car.
- 8 to 15 gallons (30–57 l) of water to run the dishwasher.
- 1.5 to 4 gallons (5.7–15 l) of water to flush the toilet once.
- 17 to 24 gallons (64–91 l) of water to take a shower or bath.
- 35 to 50 (132.5–189 l) gallons of water to wash one load of clothes in a washing machine.

the environment, the WaterSense program promotes water efficiency and pushes for the creation and use of water-efficient products, programs, and practices. WaterSense's aim is to help people learn to manage water better. The program also features a logo that will appear on products that the EPA has determined to be water-efficient. Products such as faucets and showerheads are among those that could feature the logo.

THE GREAT LAKES

Water conservation is a major issue for many states in America, particularly those states that rely on the

Great Lakes for their water supply. The Great Lakes are five large lakes located in the midwestern part of the United States. The lakes—Lake Erie, Lake Huron, Lake Michigan, Lake Superior, and Lake Ontario—contain nine-tenths of our nation's freshwater. They are the major source of drinking water to more than thirty million people living in the metropolitan areas of Chicago, Illinois; Cleveland, Ohio; Green Bay, Wisconsin; Toronto, Canada; Buffalo, New York; and the smaller suburban and rural communities that surround these metropolitan areas. Yet, only about 1 percent of the water in the Great Lakes is renewed or replaced by rain each year.

Because this freshwater supply is so valuable and massive, states around the country—even those more than a thousand miles away—with water shortage problems are attempting to tap into the Great Lakes. In reaction to this attempted water grab, eight Great Lakes states, as well as the Canadian provinces of Quebec and Ontario, have formed the Great Lakes–St. Lawrence River Basin Water Resources Compact. The compact is a multistate agreement designed to protect, con-serve, and improve the water resources of the Great Lakes–St. Lawrence River Basin and carefully monitor and restrict the ways in which the freshwater is used, diverted, and withdrawn from the system. The Great Lakes compact would build a legal wall around the lakes to ensure that none of the water is ever shipped

More than thirty million people in communities large and small depend on water from the Great Lakes, including those who live in downtown Chicago, shown here.

outside the region. States such as Arizona, and even entire continents such as Asia, are all looking for ways to access freshwater. This agreement would make it impossible for any of them to use the Great Lakes water.

The compact would also create review procedures for any new or increased uses of water in the implementation of water conservation and efficiency programs by each member state. The compact was signed in 2001 by the governors and premiers of the eight states and two Canadian provinces—Minnesota, Wisconsin, Illinois,

Indiana, Ohio, Michigan, Pennsylvania, New York, Quebec, and Ontario—that border the lakes.

The compact's member states have agreed to regulate their water use and water diversion plans and to view the agreement as an important step in preserving this natural resource. But many other states that are in desperate need of freshwater resources are outraged. They say the Great Lakes are a national resource and should not be controlled by only a few states. They argue that the system's freshwater can be used to help relieve areas that experience drought or have limited access to freshwater.

Pollution is a major environmental crisis for our freshwater supply. This pipe is emptying chemically polluted wastewater into the bed of a creek or river.

The world's rapidly growing population is a significant factor in the degradation of our water supply, but there is another equally important factor—pollution. Fortunately, pollution can be controlled and even prevented. To prevent further pollution to our water supply, it is important to understand how our freshwater bodies became polluted in the first place. There are two different sources of freshwater pollution. They are called point and nonpoint source pollution.

POINT AND NONPOINT SOURCE POLLUTION

Point source pollution is a single identifiable source of pollution. Point sources of pollution occur when harmful substances are placed directly into a body of water. Examples would include pollution introduced via oil spills, industrial waste, and sewage treatment plants. We can locate exactly where the pollution came from, which is the key difference between point and nonpoint sources of pollution.

Nonpoint source pollution comes from different places, many of which cannot be located directly. Nor can we always determine how much pollution is coming from what source. Nonpoint source pollution is caused by rainfall or snow that has melted and moved over and through the ground. As this rain and meltwater becomes runoff, it picks up and carries away natural and human-made pollutants, depositing them into lakes, rivers, wetlands, coastal waters, and even our underground sources of drinking water. Some nonpoint source pollutants include:

- Excess fertilizers, herbicides, and insecticides from agricultural lands and residential areas
- Oil, grease, and toxic chemicals from urban runoff and energy production

- Sediment from improperly managed construction sites, crop and forest lands, and eroding stream banks
- Salt from irrigation practices and acid drainage from abandoned mines
- Bacteria and nutrients from livestock, pet wastes, and faulty septic systems

The EPA reports that most states describe nonpoint source pollution as the leading cause of their water-quality problems.

Most people think water pollution comes directly from a factory or other point sources. But in the 1970s, many laws were enacted that forced businesses and industries to clean up their acts. These laws greatly reduced, and in some cases eliminated, the use of freshwater bodies as toxic dumping grounds.

Today, humans rather than industry represent the biggest source of freshwater pollution. Used motor oil poured into storm drains, soil washed from construction sites, grease from restaurants, paintbrushes cleaned in the street, or fertilizer and pesticides washed off farm fields and city lawns all enter the water supply through individual human actions. That is why it's so important for all of us to clean up our acts and learn how to prevent this type of pollution.

Freshwater bodies have an ability to break down some waste materials, but not in the quantities discarded

Polluted water endangers wildlife. These two salmon were killed when a toxic spill occurred in the waters where they lived.

by people today. Pollution can have devastating effects not only on humans, but also on animals, fish, and other organisms that rely on freshwater in order to survive.

POLLUTED FRESHWATER AND ENDANGERED WILDLIFE

As the pollution of freshwater increases, it brings with it many negative effects. Polluted freshwater is unsuitable

The World's Dirtiest Rivers

If you think that freshwater pollution is only an environmental problem in the United States, then think again. Freshwater rivers around the world are being polluted. Here are some of the worst:

- **Ganges River** (India)—This river, the most sacred river in India, is so heavily polluted with industrial and human waste that thousands of residents threatened to boycott a Hindu soul-purifying ritual that involves bathing in the river. As a result, officials in India flushed the river with water from an upstream dam.
- **Potomac River** (Maryland/Virginia)—The Potomac River flows into the Chesapeake Bay, which is surrounded by the U.S. states of Maryland and Virginia. In the fall of 2006, the appearance of intersex fish was discovered. These are fish with both male and female organs, a result of pollution-driven genetic mutation. This discovery renewed concerns about swimming, fishing, and drinking the water from the Potomac River.
- **Pripyat River** (Ukraine)—The Pripyat River passes through what is called the Zone of Alienation, a dangerous area that surrounds the Chernobyl nuclear power plant. In 1986, the power plant experienced an explosion and nuclear meltdown disaster. As a result, the Pripyat River, which flows near the reactor, became radioactive. The river is still contaminated with toxins, and a dam has been the only effective way to contain the pollution. No cleanup effort has been organized yet.
- **Songhua River** (China)—In 2005, a factory explosion in Harbin, China, dumped toxins into the Songhua River.

Almost immediately, Chinese citizens took action. After discovering that the government hid the full extent of the crisis, more than fifty thousand environmental protests and riots occurred around the country. Beijing recently pledged sixty-four million dollars to help clean up the river.

for drinking and watering our crops and plants, and it makes our lakes and rivers dirty, smelly, and dangerous to the health of all living things, including aquatic life.

Because of our carelessness, wildlife populations face the threat of increasing numbers of pollutants. In some cases, wildlife populations have faced extinction due to pollution. Wildlife, fish, and aquatic organisms living in freshwater ecosystems rely on freshwater to survive. When that water is polluted and contaminated, it can cause those animals to sicken and suffer. Some even die. Such dramatic changes can cause a massive disruption to the balance of an ecosystem.

It has recently been reported that water levels in three of the Great Lakes are far below normal. According to an article in the *New York Times*, experts expect Lake Superior, Lake Huron, and Lake Michigan to reach record-low levels. Although changes in the climate are one reason for this, experts believe that pollution is having the biggest impact.

Chinese residents from Harbin collect water from a tanker after a chemical plant explosion contaminated the Songhua River in 2005.

But there are ways to protect our water supply and keep people, wildlife, and organisms that are dependent on freshwater safe. One strategy is water purification. This is the process of removing contaminants from a water source, and it is one of the most common forms of water pollution control. Wastewater from homes, businesses, and industry is sent to water treatment plants to be treated and purified. It is then released back into streams, rivers, and lakes.

THE EPA AND THE CLEAN WATER ACT

Guiding many of the efforts to keep freshwater clean is the Clean Water Act. The growth of industry in the United States during the 1950s and '60s brought with it a level of pollution never before seen in this country. The Great Lakes were one of the many bodies of water that were becoming more and more polluted. One of the most infamous moments in water pollution history occurred when the Cuyahoga River caught fire. This event was one of the major motivating factors behind the shaping of the Clean Water Act.

The Cuyahoga River is located in northeast Ohio. It is approximately one hundred miles (161 kilometers) long and empties into Lake Erie. On June 22, 1969, industrial pollutants in the Cuyahoga River caught fire in Cleveland, Ohio, drawing national attention to environmental problems and, specifically, to water pollution. The Cuyahoga River fire lasted about thirty minutes, but it caused around fifty thousand dollars' worth of damage, mostly to railroad bridges spanning the river. It is unclear what caused the fire, but it is believed that sparks from a passing train ignited an oil slick in the river.

Because of this fire, businesses in Cleveland became infamous for their polluting practices. But this wasn't the first time that the river caught fire. The Cuyahoga River

The Cuyahoga River, located in Ohio, was so polluted it actually caught fire on June 22, 1969. It is believed that sparks from a passing train ignited the fire.

also caught fire in 1868, 1883, 1887, 1912, 1922, 1936, 1941, 1948, and 1952. The 1952 fire caused more than $1.5 million in damage.

The 1969 fire was one inspiration for the establishment of the Environmental Protection Agency (EPA) the following year. The mission of this federal agency is to protect human health and the environment by working for a cleaner, healthier environment for the American people. It does so by employing more than seventeen thousand people all across the country. Though its headquarters are in Washington, D.C., the EPA has ten regional offices located around the country and more than a dozen labs. The EPA's main purposes are to develop and enforce regulations, perform environmental research, sponsor partnerships and programs, and further environmental education.

As a result, one of the first things the EPA did was establish the Clean Water Act, which Congress passed and made into law in 1972. The Clean Water Act's main goal is to restore and maintain the integrity of our country's freshwater supply. The Clean Lakes Program, which is part of the Clean Water Act, was also established in 1972 under the section of the act called the Federal Water Pollution Control Act. The Clean Lakes Program provides financial and technical assistance to states as they work to restore lakes. The program includes suggested ways in which states can use federal funds to address the protection of lakes, ponds, and reservoirs.

Emissions from automobiles are among the pollutants that raise the temperature of our atmosphere and cause global warming.

While population growth and pollution may be two reasons why freshwater resources are in danger, many other factors account for our dwindling water supply, among them the effects of global warming, drought, overconsumption, overdevelopment, and flood control measures. As scientists continue to pinpoint the causes of global warming, and as they conduct research into its long-term impact on many aspects of planetary life, it's become clear that rising temperatures will cause sea levels to rise, weather to become more extreme, certain species of animals to become extinct, and our freshwater resources to experience drastic and negative changes.

GLOBAL WARMING

For years, scientists have been working to understand, and anticipate, the effects of global warming on our freshwater supplies. Around the world, scientists firmly believe that global warming has been a major cause of our planet's decreasing freshwater supplies. Global warming is the increase in the average temperature of Earth's air and oceans. It occurs when gases such as carbon dioxide from the tailpipes of cars and industrial smokestacks enter the atmosphere and trap heat. The heat that gets trapped ends up causing the temperatures in the air, on land, and in the sea to increase.

Global warming has affected freshwater in a number of ways, all of them negative. Ocean temperatures have risen, which has caused hurricanes to worsen since they derive energy from warm waters. An article in *National Geographic News* cites a study in the journal *Nature* that found that over the past thirty years, hurricanes and typhoons have become 50 percent stronger and are longer lasting. According to the study, these increases coincide with an increase of the sea's surface temperatures. The study suggests that if global warming continues to cause temperatures to rise, it can cause hurricane activity to increase.

Glaciers

The effect of global warming on glaciers is undeniable. Glaciers and mountain snows around the world are melting rapidly. Montana's Glacier National Park now has only twenty-seven glaciers. In 1910, the park had more than one hundred fifty. The glaciers in the Himalayas and Hindu Kush mountain ranges hold the third-largest mass of ice after Antarctica and Greenland. The rivers that these mountains feed provide water for 50 to 60 percent of the world's population. The latest survey of the mountains shows that over the past twenty-five years, the glaciers have melted faster that what was previously estimated. The United Nations Environment Program reported that the world's glaciers are melting away and that they show record losses. "Data from close to thirty reference glaciers in nine mountain ranges indicate that between the years 2004–2005 and 2005–2006 the average rate of melting and thinning more than doubled," the UNEP says in its report.

As these waters melt, the water runs off the glaciers and into the ocean. This is called glacial runoff, which also has a negative effect on water temperatures. This glacial runoff has been found to affect water currents in the Atlantic Ocean. The ocean's currents transport warm,

A Canadian inspects the Ward Hunt Ice Shelf, the largest ice shelf left in the Arctic. Scientists believe the shelf is in danger of breaking up.

surface waters toward the North and South Poles and cold, deep waters toward the equator. This movement of water helps to regulate temperatures. The extra water from glacial runoff flowing into the Atlantic Ocean could change the flow of the ocean's currents.

Ice Shelves

Global warming has also affected ice shelves. Ice shelves are thick, floating platforms of ice. They form when a glacier flows down to a coastline and onto the ocean's surface. Ice shelves are found only in Antarctica, Greenland, and Canada. The world's largest ice shelves are the Ross Ice Shelf and the Filchner-Ronne Ice Shelf. Both are located in Antarctica and are approximately the size of France.

Just recently, the Wilkins Ice Shelf collapsed in Antarctica. The ice shelf is 220 square miles (570 sq. km.). That's ten times the size of Manhattan. Scientists say the western Antarctic peninsula has warmed more than any other place on Earth over the past fifty years. The temperature has risen by 0.9 degrees Fahrenheit (0.56 degrees Celsius) each decade.

Floodplains

Floodplains are the flatlands that lie next to streams and rivers. They usually experience occasional flooding when the waters in these streams and rivers rise too high. Global warming, accompanied by torrential rain and rising seas, could bring catastrophic floods. Environmental experts predict global warming will bring drier summers and wetter winters with extreme rainfall, causing an increased risk for floods.

Drought

In a study by the journal *Science*, scientists have stated that global warming most likely made recent droughts in the United States worse than they otherwise would

A cove near Charlotte, North Carolina, normally filled with lake water, shows the results of a severe drought.

have been. They also said that global warming could increase the risk for more severe droughts in the future.

OVERCONSUMPTION AND OVERPOPULATION

Using our natural resources faster than they can be sustained and renewed is what overconsumption means. It's directly related to overpopulation, and it is measurable. The United States is the world's biggest overconsumer. With almost three hundred million people living in the United States, it is the only industrialized

World Water Monitoring Day

Adopted by the Water Environment Federation in July 2006, World Water Monitoring Day is an international outreach program that builds public awareness and involvement in protecting water resources around the world. Held annually between September 18 and October 18, the program engages communities in monitoring the condition of local rivers, streams, estuaries, and other water bodies. Since its inception in 2002, more than eighty thousand people from more than fifty countries have participated. World Water Monitoring Day challenges communities around the world to become more aware of the condition of their water quality and the impact that their behaviors have on the quality of their water resources. Conducting simple monitoring tests teaches participants about some of the most common indicators of water health and encourages further participation in more formal citizen monitoring efforts.

country that has experienced a strong population growth in the last decade. Because of this, we are placing increased stress on our natural resources. According to an article in the *Boston Globe*, Americans constitute less than 5 percent of the world's population, but we produce 25 percent of the world's carbon dioxide, consume 25 percent of the world's natural resources, and generate roughly 30 percent of the world's waste. We use three times the amount of water per capita than the world average.

OVERDEVELOPMENT

Overdevelopment has placed a major stress on our freshwater resources as well. Overdevelopment refers to the impact that urbanization, construction, and population growth has on our natural resources and the rate at which they cause significant harm to the ecosystems where this overdevelopment is occurring. Wetlands are a perfect example of the dangers of overdevelopment. Wetlands—areas of land consisting of soil that is saturated with moisture such as a swamp, marsh, or bog—are ecosystems that support the environment as a whole. Animals rely on these lands for food and water. But humans have made large-scale efforts to drain wetlands for the development of housing, malls, and business complexes. Or, we flood them for use as recreational lakes.

FLOOD CONTROL MEASURES

The effects of flood control measures can be gauged by the health of streams, rivers, and lakes. Flood control often means putting up dams to control how much water flows into an area. Dams disrupt the natural flow of rivers and streams and have many negative effects. For example, a dam cuts off the connection between a river and its floodplain, and it prevents fish such as salmon

While dams are often used to control floods, they disrupt the natural flow of rivers, negatively impacting the fish and wildlife that live in and around the riverbeds.

from swimming upstream to spawn or lay eggs. Dams also change the biology of an area. Plants that rely on a larger volume of water to live have trouble surviving, as do certain kinds of fish and wildlife that rely on the shelter and nutrients provided by freshwater flora.

Suburban sprawl is pushing farther and farther into the desert, as with this community in Las Vegas, Nevada, where water supplies are already limited.

While understanding freshwater and threats to its supply can be complicated, the economics behind it are very simple. It's a clear case of supply and demand. There is a limited supply of freshwater, but the demand is growing and growing. At some point, something has to change or the supply will not exist anymore. Because our planet cannot replenish freshwater fast enough to satisfy the ever-growing need, humans must reduce their demands on freshwater resources. As populations continue to grow, however, there doesn't seem to be a point in the foreseeable future when demand will slow down.

POPULATION BOOMS AND SHRINKING WATER RESOURCES

Geography is playing a major role in the dwindling of the world's freshwater resources. It is estimated that by the year 2025, more than three billion people will live in locations where it will be difficult, or even impossible, to get enough freshwater to satisfy their needs, the needs of their communities, and the needs of the industries that will help to sustain these newly populated areas. Parts of the United States are already experiencing stress on water resources as communities spring up in areas that have little access to freshwater sources. Some of our nation's fastest-growing cities, including San Antonio, Texas; Las Vegas, Nevada; and Phoenix, Arizona, are located in the nation's driest climates. This population growth forces communities to look elsewhere for water. But that doesn't mean other communities, with shrinking water resources of their own, are ready to share.

In Texas, the Edwards Aquifer, a major underground water source, supplies most of central Texas, including the city of San Antonio, with freshwater. The aquifer is being emptied faster than rainwater can replenish it. Many cattle ranchers in Texas are angry because they use the aquifer's water for their farms and livestock. Las Vegas has projected that it will triple in population by the middle of the twenty-first century. It also estimates that the city will run out of water as early as 2020 if the current water usage rates remain the same. That's just a few years away. Las Vegas has few options since it is located in a desert. The idea of building a dam and a reservoir in Utah's Virgin River Canyon has been proposed, but it faces severe opposition from environmentalists, who say that water from the canyon supports local communities and wildlife.

Arizona has already put in place a statewide conservation program called Water—Use It Wisely. A number of cities in the state—including Mesa, Phoenix, Tempe, Scottsdale, Chandler, Peoria, Glendale, Avondale, Safford, and the towns of Gilbert and Prescott Valley—are participating in the promotion. The campaign informs the public about how simple steps can dramatically reduce one's use of water. Some measures are as simple as soaking pots and pans to loosen grease and food particles instead of running the kitchen sink while you scrub them clean. Other tips include how to water lawns most efficiently. The campaign spread quickly throughout the state and gained the attention of the Home Depot Company. All forty of Home Depot's stores

Owens Lake was the first major water diversion project designed to bring freshwater to Los Angeles, California. The lake no longer exists.

in Arizona carry water conservation products and hold in-store workshops to teach people how to use these products correctly.

Finding water for growing populations is a challenge. Water diversion projects have already drained major bodies of water. Owens Lake, the first major project to bring water to Los Angeles, California, doesn't exist anymore. Even worse, the EPA has estimated that what's left of it, mostly dust from the lake bottom, is the largest single source of airborne particulate pollution in the country. The Colorado River has experienced its own problems, too, as a result of water diversion. The river has been so heavily drained by the farms and growing cities of the Southwestern United States that during most months of the year, there isn't enough water flow to reach the Pacific Ocean, into which the river ordinarily empties.

Globally, the picture gets more grim. Some experts believe that as competition for water increases, it could cause regional wars in the coming years. Three countries in the Middle East—Iraq, Syria, and Turkey—have already verbally threatened one another over their use of shared rivers. Historians believed that future wars will not be fought over philosophical disagreements, ethnicity, political and social freedom, or independence, which were the key themes of major conflicts such as the U.S. Civil War, World War I, and World War II. Instead, wars will be waged over land, water, and natural resources as countries struggle to provide the most basic needs for their citizens.

As global warming affects our climate and weather, that in turn will affect our freshwater resources. Climate changes are an impending threat that could make it more difficult for water to replenish itself naturally. If predictions of drastic climate change are true, then more unpredictable weather will bring more droughts. Freshwater resources will be less likely to be replenished, and some portions of the world could turn into deserts. Droughts are already impacting freshwater supplies in states including Florida, Georgia, and California. Florida's Lake Okeechobee, which supplies South Florida with freshwater, is dangerously low. So much of the lakebed is dry that more than twelve thousand acres of it caught fire in June 2007.

THE SUSTAINABLE RIVERS PROJECT

The Nature Conservancy is working with dam engineers and flood management agencies to restore some of the natural flood patterns in rivers. They are also protecting communities and wildlife living near a number of rivers that need to be restored or preserved. According to the Nature Conservancy's Web site, it and the U.S. Army Corps of Engineers formed a partnership in July 2002 to restore and preserve rivers across the country. "Under the Sustainable Rivers Project, the Conservancy and the Corps have been working together to improve dam management in order to protect the ecological health of rivers and surrounding natural areas while continuing to provide services such as flood control and power generation," the site explains.

One river that is getting a much-needed boost is the Green River in Kentucky. The Green River is the nation's fourth-most-diverse river for fish and mussel species. The Conservancy and the Army Corps identified a better water-release schedule for the Green River Dam. They found that by delaying dam releases until after the spawning period for certain fish and mussel species, they could avoid disrupting this crucial time for fish reproduction.

The Sustainable Rivers Project currently is working on eleven rivers. These rivers, which have a total of

World Water Day: A Global Conservation Effort

The idea for World Water Day was first introduced during the 1992 United Nations Conference on Environment and Development in Rio de Janeiro, Brazil. Also called the Earth Summit, the conference is held each year and raises awareness of environmental issues around the world.

In a speech commemorating the event, then-UN Secretary General Kofi Annan stressed how much our global community has taken freshwater resources for granted. World Water Day was created to help governments, key partners such as education ministries and schools, civil society organizations, and communities and individuals worldwide to achieve their goals in freshwater conservation. The event's Web site provides links to the world's best online water information and practical water conservation advice, suggestions for local and regional activities, and high-resolution posters, logos, and photos to help groups and individuals promote and participate in the day.

twenty-six dams, flow through thirteen states. The conservancy is planning on adding more rivers and dams to the project in the future.

FRESHWATER AND THE DEVELOPING WORLD

Unsafe water and sanitation leads to more than 80 percent of all diseases in the developing world. The term "developing world" refers to countries that have few

In the developing world, more than one billion people lack access to freshwater. These African children, who live in the Darfur region in Sudan, collect their only source of water—rainwater—for drinking and cooking.

factories. People in these countries earn low wages and have a very low standard of living. In contrast, developed countries like the United States, Canada, and many European nations have comparatively strong economic systems and industrial growth.

In the developing world, more than one billion people lack access to freshwater resources, and more than two billion people still need access to basic sanitation facilities. The United Nations has established a number of development goals for these countries. One in particular is sustainable water and sanitation. The UN is working to reduce by more than half the number of people worldwide who do not have access to clean water.

To help offset water pollution, modern water treatment plants are working overtime to help purify water.

As global warming, pollution, overpopulation, and overdevelopment all take their toll on our freshwater resources, there are ways that we can decontaminate and protect our water supply and use water more efficiently. We can do things to treat contaminated water to make it usable, conserve and use less water, and be more efficient in how we use water. Since freshwater supplies are not growing, and demand is not lessening, we need to find creative ways to make the most of our available stores of water.

CARBON FILTRATION

The most popular water treatment method is to clean water through carbon filtration. Still the best known and most reliable of water treatment methods, carbon filtration dates to the 1700s. A piece of activated carbon is placed in contaminated water and a positive charge is sent through the carbon. The carbon then attracts contaminants and impurities from the water. Carbon absorption is now one of the fastest-growing components of the water treatment market, with increases of 86 percent for domestic applications and 26 percent in industrial applications since 1990.

A member of the Bangladesh Army uses a portable water purification machine that can purify 264 gallons (1,000 liters) of water an hour.

WATER PURIFICATION

Most water that we drink is purified. But water purification may also be used for a number of other purposes, including for medication and industrial applications. There are even portable water purification methods that can be used to treat unsafe water by removing chlorine, bad taste, heavy metals such as lead and mercury, and odors from the water. Portable water purification methods are used in developing countries that need easy and inexpensive ways to clean water.

ULTRAVIOLET LIGHT

Sunlight quickly destroys bacteria and viruses and is a natural way to clean freshwater. Since the early 1900s, human-made ultraviolet lights have been used for cleaning water. In 1966, the U.S. Department of Health, Education, and Welfare recognized that this technology can be used in large-scale water treatment methods. Water treated with ultraviolet light is free of most bacteria and viruses, and there are no chemical additives as a result of the process.

ION EXCHANGE

Also called water softeners, ion exchange continues to be the most effective treatment option for eliminating certain minerals from freshwater. Hard water is water that contains high levels of calcium or magnesium. The idea behind a water softener is simple: the calcium and magnesium ions in the water are replaced with sodium ions. Companies have been selling more and more softeners since 1990. In fact, sales of water softeners have increased by 56 percent.

BOILING

The easiest and least expensive way to clean water is to boil it. Boiling is the best method to make water safe to drink. Boiling water kills bacteria found in water drawn from rivers and lakes.

INNOVATIVE LAKE AND RIVER RESTORATION

The Nature Conservancy has created the Great Rivers Partnership with corporations from around the world. According to the Nature Conservancy Web site, the partnership "is dedicated to the conservation of the world's great river systems for the benefit of the people and the species that depend upon them for life." The partnership works to rescue some of the world's most damaged freshwater systems and change the way that large river systems are preserved and protected. The Conservancy's partners include Caterpillar, Inc., a leading manufacturer of construction and mining equipment; IBM, a worldwide computer technology company; and the McKnight Foundation, which is devoted to improving the quality of life for individuals, families, and whole communities and is one of the largest foundations in the United States. These partners, among others, all have an interest in conserving, maintaining, and restoring our freshwater rivers.

The purpose of the partnership is to create a new model for sustaining the world's great river systems and the plants, animals, and people that depend on them. Great rivers are defined as rivers with seasonal floods that are sufficiently long-lasting, predictable, and extensive. The rivers the partnership will help are the Mississippi River in the United States, Brazil's Paraguay-Paraná River system, and China's Yangtze River.

Beginning with these three rivers, and eventually expanding to include other great rivers, the Conservancy has initiated a plan to conserve, restore, and sustain the development of these important ecosystems.

CORPORATE RESPONSIBILITY

Of all the freshwater that is consumed, 98 percent is used by industry. Companies add water to products and use it to manufacture products, run machinery, and transport products internationally. Given how important freshwater sources are to their businesses, some companies are responding to the freshwater crisis by reducing their use of water.

Ensuring the Future of Freshwater

Freshwater Future is a nonprofit organization that provides financial assistance, communications and networking assistance, and technical assistance to individual citizens and more than 1,800 grassroots watershed groups working throughout the Great Lakes basin. These groups protect and restore the rivers, lakes, and wetlands in their communities.

One of the groups that Freshwater Future has assisted is the Glindo Earth Force, a group of students from the Walnut Creek Middle School in Millcreek Township near Erie, Pennsylvania. Having learned of some nonpoint pollution that was contaminating nearby Lake Erie and Presque Isle Bay and that was caused by urban runoff from streets and parking lots, the students of Walnut Creek Middle School collected and examined sludge from their town's gutters, sewers, and catch basins. What they found in the sludge were deposits of lead, cadmium, and other metals and harsh industrial solvents, oil, and grease. Further research led them to conclude that something as simple as weekly street sweeping could reduce pollutants by as much as 25–50 percent. Yet, Millcreek Township only sweeps its streets about once or twice a year. The Glindo Earth Force is currently trying to convince the township to increase its street-sweeping activities, while also educating the public about the dangers to freshwater posed by automobiles that leak oil and other fluids.

Freshwater Future helped clean up Presque Isle Bay further when it supported the efforts of some Strong Vincent High School students who sought to locate the mysterious source of pollution that was causing tumors and discolorations in the Brown Bullhead fish population. Using extensive water and soil sampling, the students located the creek in Erie County that was funneling the pollutants into the bay. They then backtracked to discover the source itself: contaminated soil that, during heavy rains, was eroding and washing into the nearby creek and out into the bay. The problem was solved by removing the contaminated soil, stabilizing the bank, and creating an anti-erosion buffer zone between this bank and the creek.

Again with the assistance of Freshwater Future, other Erie, Pennsylvania, area teenagers helped to prevent parking lot runoff from polluting local freshwater sources. They successfully lobbied the city to allow them to plan a "rain garden" beside the parking lot, where it could intercept and filter polluted runoff. The flowers and shrubs planted by the teens would catch and filter storm water runoff, removing pollutants before sending the water down the storm drains and into local Mill Creek and, eventually, from there into Lake Erie. The students then offered tours of the rain garden and taught visitors how they could create their own pollution-trapping flowering oases.

Kentucky's Green River is part of the Sustainable Rivers Project, which aims to restore and preserve rivers across the United States.

E. Neville Isdell, chief executive officer of the Coca-Cola Company, announces the company's plan to fund a twenty-million-dollar project to conserve seven rivers worldwide, as well as reduce its own pollution and water usage amounts.

The Coca-Cola Company

This soda giant is one of the world's leading manufacturers of soft drinks and bottled water. The Coca-Cola Company has pledged to replace the water it uses to create its beverages. The company will focus its actions in three core areas: reducing the water used to produce its beverages, recycling water used for beverage manufacturing processes, and replenishing water in communities and nature. The company made the announcement at an annual meeting of the World Wildlife Federation (WWF), where Coca-Cola launched a partnership with WWF to conserve and protect freshwater resources. This commitment from Coca-Cola will be used to help conserve seven of the world's most important freshwater river basins, support more efficient water management in its operations, and reduce the company's carbon footprint.

InterContinental Hotel Group

A large corporation that owns hotel properties around the world, including Holiday Inn, Candlewood Suites, and Crown Plaza, the InterContinental Hotel Group has developed the Conserving for Tomorrow program. The program asks guests to use their linens and towels more than once to save on water, detergent, energy, labor, and replacement linen. For each average-sized one-hundred-room hotel, it saves 5,812 gallons (22,000 liters) of water and 40 gallons (150 liters) of detergent each month. The program has an 80–90 percent approval rating from hotel guests.

Home Depot

The home improvement superstore has partnered with EPA's WaterSense Program to promote water-efficient products and practices around the country. The company sells these products in all of its stores and holds in-store workshops on how to use them. To date the company has sold more than 190,000 water conservation products. Home Depot's Web site also lists ways in which people can conserve more water both in and around their homes.

Nestlé

This food manufacturing company has some of the most famous products in the world, including KitKat candy bars, Nesquik chocolate milk, and Purina pet food. Over the past few years, the company has reduced the amount of water that it uses in its manufacturing operations, even though production of the company's products has increased. Nestlé's goal is to continue reducing the amount of water it uses and remain as environmentally friendly as possible.

General Electric

The company that makes lightbulbs, television sets, and appliances such as your refrigerator and stove has been at the forefront of conserving water. Among General Electric's advances are water purification technologies that result in the purification and reuse of 90 percent of industrial wastewater. The company has also made a commitment to maintain its level of water usage, although it is producing more and more products each year. GE is even helping other companies do more with less. Ford Motor Company contacted GE when it was having trouble managing wastewater at a truck plant in Kentucky. With GE's help, Ford was able to reduce the plant's water usage by 230,400 gallons (872,159 liters) a year.

PULLING TOGETHER

There is a growing urgency to not only preserve freshwater resources, but also to use these resources better. Using less water for everything from brushing our teeth and washing our dishes, to watering our crops and powering our industries, is a major concern. We need to slow our current use of water so that we can replenish freshwater supplies. Right now, we use more water than nature can replenish naturally. With no way to help create more water, it's the responsibility of everyone—people, companies, cities, states, and countries worldwide—to get involved and begin to make water conservation a major priority.

GLOSSARY

aquifers An aquifer is an underground layer of water-bearing permeable rock or unconsolidated materials (gravel, sand, silt, or clay) from which groundwater can be usefully extracted using a water well.

conservation The preservation or protection of something.

contamination The process of making something less pure.

environmentalist A person who advocates on behalf of the environment.

estuary A water passage in which an ocean tide meets a river current.

evaporation The conversion of water into vapor.

glacier A large body of ice moving slowly down a slope or valley or spreading outward on a land surface.

ice shelf A thick, floating platform of ice that forms when a glacier or ice sheet flows down to a coastline and onto the ocean surface.

particulate pollution Tiny particles of solid or liquid pollution that are suspended in the air.

preservation The act of saving and protecting something, like the natural environment.

purification The process of rendering something pure.

restoration Bringing something back to its former condition or state.

Freshwater Future
P.O. Box 2479
Petoskey, MI 49770-2479
(231) 348-8200
Web site: http://glhabitat.org
Freshwater Future is a nonprofit organization that builds
community-based citizen action to protect and
restore the water quality of the Great Lakes basin.

Freshwater Society
2500 Shadywood Road
Excelsior, MN 55331
(952) 471-9773
Web site: http://www.freshwater.org
The Freshwater Society is a leading public, nonprofit
organization dedicated to conserving, restoring, and
protecting freshwater resources and their surrounding
watersheds.

National Water Research Institute
Environment Canada
867 Lakeshore Road
P.O. Box 5050
Burlington, ON L7R 4A6
Canada

The National Water Research Institute is Canada's largest freshwater research facility.

Nature Conservancy
4245 North Fairfax Drive, Suite 100
Arlington, VA 22203-1606
(703) 841-5300
Web site: http://www.nature.org
The Nature Conservancy is a leading conservation organization that works around the world to protect important lands and waters.

WEB SITES

Due to the changing nature of Internet links, Rosen Publishing has developed an online list of Web sites related to the subject of this book. This site is updated regularly. Please use this link to access this list:

http://www.rosenlinks.com/eet/ned

FOR FURTHER READING

Dempsey, Dave. *On the Brink: The Great Lakes in the 21st Century*. East Lansing, MI: Michigan State University Press, 2004.

Desoni, Dana. *Hydrosphere: Freshwater Systems and Pollution*. New York, NY: Chelsea House Publications, 2008.

Flannery, Tim. *The Weather Makers: How Man Is Changing the Climate and What It Means for Life on Earth*. New York, NY: Atlantic Monthly Press, 2006.

Gleick, Peter H. *The World's Water 2006–2007: The Biennial Report on Freshwater Resources*. Washington, DC: Island Press, 2006.

Kolbert, Elizabeth. *Field Notes from a Catastrophe*. New York, NY: Bloomsbury USA, 2006.

Linden, Eugene. *The Winds of Change: Climate, Weather, and the Destruction of Civilizations*. New York, NY: Simon & Schuster, 2007.

Pearce, Fred. *Keepers of the Spring: Reclaiming Our Waters in an Age of Globalization*. Washington, DC: Island Press, 2004.

Raines Ward, Diane. *Water Wars*. New York, NY: Riverhead Trade, 2003.

Spring, Barbara. *The Dynamic Great Lakes*. Cambridge, England: Independence Books, 2002.

BIBLIOGRAPHY

Anin, Peter. *The Great Lakes Water Wars*. Washington, DC: Island Press, 2006.

Barringer, Felicity. "Water Levels in 3 Great Lakes Dip Far Below Normal." *New York Times*, August 14, 2007. Retrieved March 28, 2008 (http://www.nytimes.com/2007/08/14/us/14lakes.html?_r=1&adxnnl=1&oref=slogin&adxnnlx=1207062274-z/vq2IINJPjf+GUJikJWrw).

Cauchon, Dennis. "Great Lakes Compact at the Center of Great Debate." *USA Today*, December 10, 2006. Retrieved March 27, 2008 (http://www.usatoday.com/news/nation/2006-12-10-great-lakes-debate_x.htm).

CNN.com. "Bill Aims to Shore Up Clean Water Act." April 12, 2000. Retrieved March 26, 2008 (http://archives.cnn.com/2000/NATURE/04/12/water.bill.enn/index.html).

Donnelly, John. "Alarm Sounds on U.S. Population Boom." Boston.com, August 31, 2006. Retrieved March 26, 2008 (http://www.boston.com/news/nation/washington/articles/2006/08/31/alarm_sounds_on_us_population_boom).

NationalGeographic.com. "Global Warming Fast Facts." June 14, 2007. Retrieved March 29, 2008 (http://news.nationalgeographic.com/news/2004/12/1206_041206_global_warming.html).

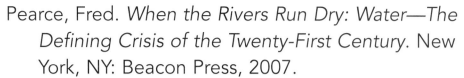
Pearce, Fred. *When the Rivers Run Dry: Water—The Defining Crisis of the Twenty-First Century.* New York, NY: Beacon Press, 2007.

Roach, John. "Is Global Warming Making Hurricanes Worse?" NationalGeographic.com, August 4, 2005. Retrieved March 30, 2008 (http://news.nationalgeographic.com/news/2005/08/0804_050804_hurricanewarming.html).

Salemme, Elizabeth. "The World's Dirty Rivers." *Time*, January 22, 2007. Retrieved March 30, 2008 (http://www.time.com/time/health/article/0,8599,1581251,00.html).

Shiva, Vandana. *Water Wars: Privatization, Pollution, and Profit.* Cambridge, MA: South End Press, 2002.

Spotts, Peter N. "A Cautionary Picture of Water Supplies as Earth Warms." *Christian Science Monitor*, November 17, 2005. Retrieved March 30, 2008 (http://www.csmonitor.com/2005/1117/p04s01-usgn.html).

Stevens, William K. "On the Climate Change Beat, Doubt Gives Way to Certainty." *New York Times*, February 6, 2007. Retrieved March 28, 2008 (http://www.nytimes.com/2007/02/06/science/earth/06clim.html?_r=1&oref=slogin).

Water Education Foundation. "How Much Water Does It Take To . . ." Retrieved March 28, 2008 (http://www.water-ed.org/kids.asp#WaterPollutionNoKnows).

INDEX

A

aquifers, 9, 38–39

C

carbon filtration, 46
carbon footprint, 53
Clean Lakes Program, 27
Clean Water Act, 25–27
Coca-Cola Company, 52–53
condensation, 11
Cuyahoga River fires, 25–26

D

drinking water, safe, 4, 5–6, 8, 19,
    21, 23, 43–44, 46–47, 48

E

Earth Summit, 43
Environmental Protection Agency
    (EPA), 9, 13–14, 20, 26–27,
    40, 53
environmentalists, 12, 39
estuaries, 34

F

Federal Water Pollution Control
    Act, 27
flood control/management, 6, 22,
    35–37, 42–43
floodplains, 32, 35
Foundation for Water and Energy
    Education, 10

freshwater
    and agriculture, 5–6, 8, 12, 19,
        21, 23, 39, 40, 55
    conserving of, 6, 13–17, 39–40,
        43, 45, 53–55
    and drought, 17, 28, 32–33, 41
    ecosystems, 9, 23, 35
    and geography, 6, 14–17, 38–44
    and global warming, 26–33, 41, 45
    growing demand for, 6, 11–14,
        37, 45
    and industry, 5–6, 7, 12, 19, 20,
        24, 25, 38, 43–44, 46, 49,
        52–55
    and overconsumption, 6, 28,
        33–34, 39–40, 45, 53
    and overdevelopment, 6, 20, 28,
        35, 45
    pollution of, 6, 18–27, 40, 45,
        50–51
    preservation of, 7, 25–27
    replenishment of, 7, 9, 10–11, 37,
        52–53, 55
    sources of, 5–6, 7, 9, 11, 14–17, 41
    treatment methods, 24, 46–48, 54
    and wildlife, 4, 9, 21, 22, 23, 24,
        28–29, 35, 36, 42, 50
    and world population, 6, 12, 18,
        28, 37–38
Freshwater Future, 50–51

G

General Electric, 54–55
glacial runoff, 30–31

glaciers, 5, 9, 30–31
global warming, 26–33, 41, 45
Great Lakes, 14–17, 23, 25, 50
Great Rivers Partnership, 48–49
groundwater, 11

H

Home Depot, 39–40, 53–54
hydrologic cycle, 10–11

I

ice shelves, 9, 31–32
InterContinental Hotel Group, 53
ion exchange, 47–48
irrigation, 20

M

meltwater, 19

N

National Geographic, 5, 29
Nature, 29
Nature Conservancy, 12, 42, 48
Nestlé, 54

O

overpopulation, 12–13, 45

P

point/nonpoint source pollution,
    18–21, 50
polar ice caps, 5, 9
precipitation, 11

R

renewable resources, defined, 6
rivers, world's dirtiest, 22

S

salt water, 6, 8, 9
Science, 32
Sustainable Rivers Project, 42–43

U

ultraviolet light, 47
United Nations Conference on
    Environment and
    Development, 43
United Nations Environment
    Program (UNEP), 30
urban runoff, 50–51
urbanization, 35
U.S. Army Corp of Engineers, 42
U.S. Congress, 27
U.S. Department of Health,
    Education, and Welfare, 47

W

wastewater, 24, 54
Water Environment Federation, 34
WaterSense, 13–14, 53
wetlands, 5, 6, 7, 19, 35, 50
World Water Day, 43
World Water Monitoring Day, 34
World Wildlife Federation (WWF), 53

ABOUT THE AUTHOR

Laura La Bella is a writer and editor. She lives and works in Rochester, New York, with her husband, Matthew, a social studies teacher. Since writing this book, La Bella and her husband have been working to reduce their own water usage by exercising water conservation techniques.

PHOTO CREDITS

Cover Skip Brown/National Geographic/Getty Images; p. 1 Andy Nelson/ Christian Science Monitor/Getty Images; pp. 4–5 © www.istockphoto.com/ ooyoo; p. 8 © www.istockphoto.com/Linda Armstrong; p. 10 NOAA; p. 13 © www.istockphoto.com/adisa; p. 16 © www.istockphoto.com/Ian McDonnell; p. 18 David Woodfall/Stone/Getty Images; p. 21 Natalie Fobes/Stone/Getty Images; p. 24 Peter Parks/AFP/Getty Images; pp. 26, 31, 52 © AP Images; p. 28 © www.istockphoto.com/David Parsons; p. 33 Davis Turner/Getty Images; p. 36 © www.istockphoto.com/Andrew Zarivny; p. 37 Todd Bigelow/ Aurora/Getty Images; p. 40 Gordon Wiltsie/National Geographic/Getty Images; p. 44 © Moses Muiruri/Reuters/Landov; p. 45 © www.istockphoto. com/Tomasz Szymanski; p. 46 © Zaid Islam/Drik/Majority World/The Image Works; p. 51 © Lynda Richardson.

Designer: Tom Forget; Photo Researcher: Amy Feinberg